All New Crafts for Thanksgiving

KATHY ROSS

illustrated by Sharon Lane Holm

Millbrook Press

Minneapolis

For Joe and Ellie
—K.R.

For Wink and Ron, thanks!
—S.L.H.

Millbrook Press
A division of Lerner Publishing Group
241 First Avenue North
Minneapolis, Minnesota 55401 U.S.A.

Website address: www.lernerbooks.com

Library of Congress Cataloging-in-Publication Data

Ross, Kathy (Katharine Reynolds), 1948–
    All new crafts for Thanksgiving / Kathy Ross; illustrated by Sharon Lane Holm.
       p.   cm. — (All new holiday crafts for kids)
    ISBN 13: 978–0–7613–2922–0 (lib. bdg.)
    ISBN 10: 0–7613–2922–6 (lib. bdg.)
    1. Thanksgiving decorations—Juvenile literature. 2. Handicraft—Juvenile literature.
    [1. Thanksgiving decorations. 2. Handicraft.] I. Holm, Sharon Lane, ill. II. Title.
    TT900.T5R65 2006
    745.594'1649—dc22   2003023090

Manufactured in the United States of America

1 2 3 4 5 6 – DP – 11 10 09 08 07 06

Contents

A long time ago some people came all the way from England to America on a ship called the *Mayflower*.

Sailing Ship Cup

Here is what you need:

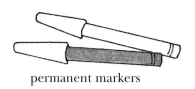

permanent markers

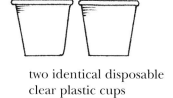

two identical disposable
clear plastic cups

Here is what you do:

1 Use the permanent markers to draw a picture of a ship like
the *Mayflower* on one side of one of the cups.

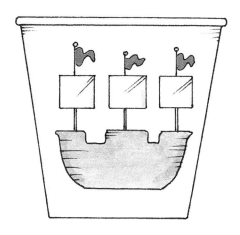 

2 Color water all the way around the outside of the second
cup. You might want to draw a sun at the top edge
of the cup.

3 Place the ship cup inside the water cup. Sail the ship by turning the outer cup around while holding the top rim of the inner cup.

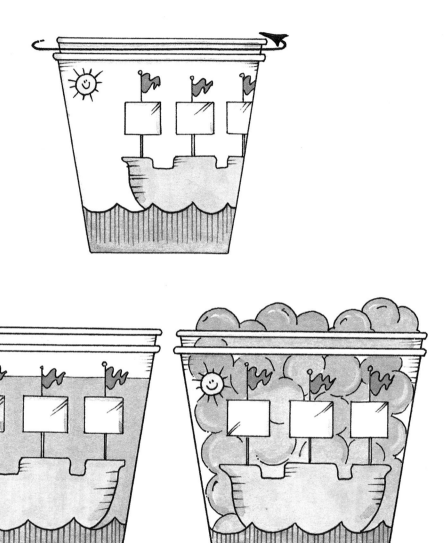

"Sailing ship" cups can be used to serve food such as pudding or gelatin salad or cranberries. You could also use them as favors on your Thanksgiving table, filling them with small toys or candies.

The people who came to America on the
Mayflower **were called Pilgrims.**

Girl Pilgrim Sleeve Puppe

Here is what you need:

scissors

two wiggle eyes

ruler

piece of red pipe cleaner

thin craft ribbo

small pom-pom

yarn bits for hair

glue

old light-colored sock

stretchy glove

discarded man's shirt

white craft glue

white fabric

rubber band

fiberfill

Here is what you do:

1 Cut a 1-foot (30-cm) piece from the sleeve of the shirt for the dress and hat of the puppet.

2 Cut half of the foot part off the end of the sock. Stuff the toe with fiberfill to make the head for the puppet. Close the open end using the rubber band.

3 With the shirt cuff buttoned, push the head up in the sleeve so that it shows through the opening of the cuff. Fold back the edges of the cuff to look like the rim of a bonnet. Glue the head in place.

4 Make a bow from the craft ribbon. Glue it on the cuff where the two ends meet, to look like the bow of the bonnet. This will be the bottom of the puppet's face. Glue yarn bits around the rim of the bonnet for hair.

5 Glue the two wiggle eyes on the face. Glue the pom-pom below the eyes for a nose. Bend the piece of red pipe cleaner into a smile, and glue it in place for the mouth.

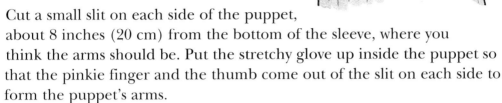

6 Cut a small slit on each side of the puppet, about 8 inches (20 cm) from the bottom of the sleeve, where you think the arms should be. Put the stretchy glove up inside the puppet so that the pinkie finger and the thumb come out of the slit on each side to form the puppet's arms.

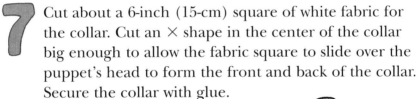

7 Cut about a 6-inch (15-cm) square of white fabric for the collar. Cut an × shape in the center of the collar big enough to allow the fabric square to slide over the puppet's head to form the front and back of the collar. Secure the collar with glue.

8 Cut a rectangle of white fabric for the apron. Glue the apron to the front of the puppet, gathering the top part slightly.

9 Tie a piece of ribbon around the puppet for the apron tie. Glue it to the top of the apron and tie the ends in a bow behind the puppet. Do not tie it so tight that you will be unable to get your hand inside the puppet.

To use the puppet, place your hand in the glove inside the puppet and use your center finger to tip the head forward. What do you think this Pilgrim puppet might say about the first Thanksgiving?

**Like all people, the Pilgrims had both happy times
and times when they were sad or afraid.**

Changing Face Boy Pilgrim

Here is what you need:

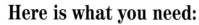

scissors

white craft glue

permanent markers

masking tape

black construction paper

gold sparkle stem

three identical white Styrofoam

one blue plastic cup the same
size as the white cups

Here is what you do:

1 Stack the three white Styrofoam cups together
and turn them upside down.

2 Use the permanent markers to draw eyes on
the top rim, a nose on the middle rim, and a
mouth on the bottom rim.

3 About a third of the way around the cups,
draw a different set of eyes, nose, and
mouth.

4 Finally, about another third of the way
around, draw a third set of eyes, nose,
and mouth that are different from the
first two faces.

5 Turn the blue cup upside down to become the hat. Wrap masking tape around the rim of the hat for the hatband. You can leave the tape brown or color it with a permanent marker.

6 Fold a piece of the gold sparkle stem into a square for the hat buckle. Glue the buckle to the hatband.

7 Trace around the rim of the blue cup on the black paper. Then cut a circle of black paper about 1 inch (2.5 cm) wider than the outer rim of the blue cup.

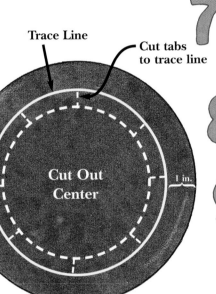

Trace Line

Cut tabs to trace line

Cut Out Center

1 in.

8 Cut out the center of the circle, cutting about 1/4 inch (.6 cm) inside the trace line.

9 Cut tabs around the inside of the circle to the traced line. Fold the tabs upward and slide the ring of black paper over the top white cup to form a hat brim.

10 Dab some glue on the tabs, then slide the blue cup hat over the top white cup.

To change the mood of the Pilgrim puppet, turn the white cups to make various combinations of facial features to express different feelings.

The Pilgrims might have starved if they had not received help from the Native Americans already living in America.

Native-American Headband

Here is what you need:

white craft glue

scissors

corrugated cardboard

glue

ruler

seed beads

rickrack

two paper fasteners

craft feathers

pencil

hole punch

rubber band

Here is what you do:

1 Cut a strip of corrugated cardboard about 1 1/2 inches (3.75 cm) wide and 15 inches (38 cm) long for the headband. Make sure that the grooves in the cardboard run from top to bottom on the band.

15"

2 Punch a hole in each end of the band. Put a paper fastener in each hole and bend the tabs to secure.

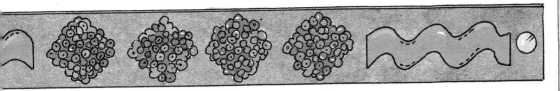

3 Flatten the band and decorate it by gluing on seed beads and rickrack.

4 When the glue has dried, close the headband by slipping the rubber band around the paper fasteners.

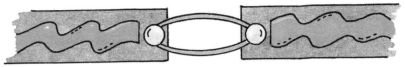

5 Slide craft feathers into the holes created by the grooves at the top of the band.

To make the headband smaller or larger, just change the length of the rubber band.

**The Native Americans showed the Pilgrims
how to grow corn to eat.**

Indian-Corn Pin

Here is what you need:

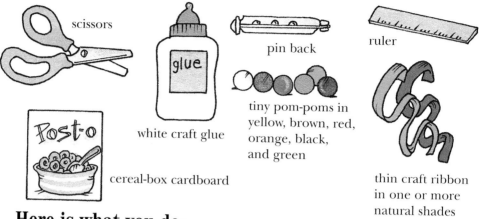

scissors

pin back

ruler

white craft glue

tiny pom-poms in
yellow, brown, red,
orange, black,
and green

cereal-box cardboard

thin craft ribbon
in one or more
natural shades

Here is what you do:

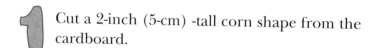

1 Cut a 2-inch (5-cm) -tall corn shape from the
cardboard.

2 Glue the tiny pom-poms all over the corn shape
to look like colorful corn kernels.

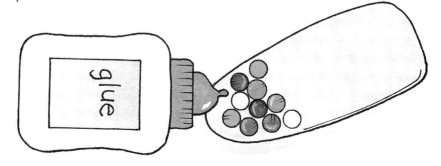

3 Cut several strips of thin ribbon to glue across the back and on both sides of the front of the corn to look like the husk.

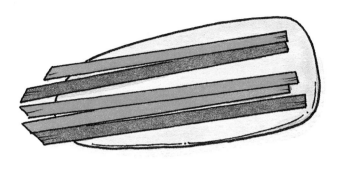

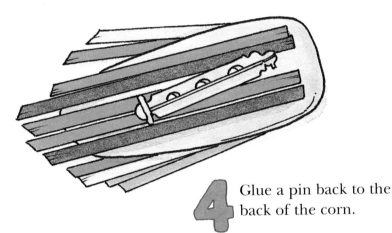

4 Glue a pin back to the back of the corn.

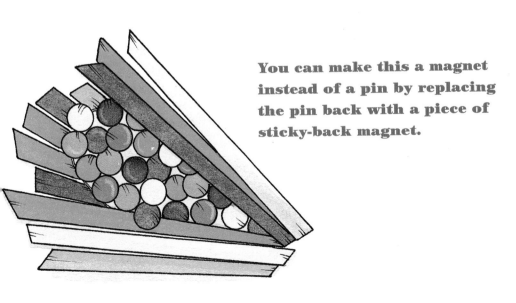

You can make this a magnet instead of a pin by replacing the pin back with a piece of sticky-back magnet.

The Pilgrims and the Native Americans joined together to celebrate and give thanks for having enough food for the winter.

Pilgrims and Native Americans Together

Here is what you need:

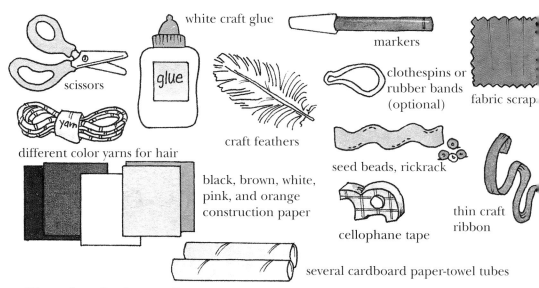

scissors

white craft glue

glue

markers

clothespins or rubber bands (optional)

fabric scrap

craft feathers

different color yarns for hair

seed beads, rickrack

black, brown, white, pink, and orange construction paper

thin craft ribbon

cellophane tape

several cardboard paper-towel tubes

Here is what you do:

1 You should make at least four figures for the grouping, but more can be added. Cut the tubes so that you will have two adults and two children. Make the adults slightly different heights.

2 To make Pilgrims, wrap the tubes in black construction paper and glue in place. For the man, wrap a band of pink paper around the tube for the face, leaving part of the black tube showing at the top for the hat. Glue a strip of black paper across the front of the hat for the brim. Use markers to draw the face. Glue on yarn bits for hair. Add details such as a white paper collar and a ribbon hatband.

3 For the girl Pilgrim, wrap a strip of pink paper around the top of the tube for the head. Use markers to draw a face on the

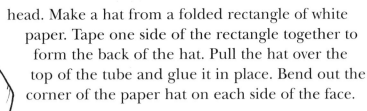

head. Make a hat from a folded rectangle of white paper. Tape one side of the rectangle together to form the back of the hat. Pull the hat over the top of the tube and glue it in place. Bend out the corner of the paper hat on each side of the face.

4 Cut a collar from the white paper and glue it on the top of the dress. Glue a ribbon bow at the chin of the Pilgrim. Glue bits of yarn around the face for hair.

5 To make the Native Americans, wrap the tubes in brown paper. Wrap the top of each tube with a strip of orange paper for the head. Use markers to draw a face on the head.

6 Glue long strands of black yarn over the top opening of the tube and hanging down the sides and back of the head. You might want to try doing braids for the girl. Use craft ribbon to make a headband. Tuck a craft feather in the headband.

7 Decorate the boy with seed beads and rickrack. Wrap the girl in a fabric scrap for a cozy blanket.

8 Glue all the figures together with the adults in back and the children in front. You might want to use clothespins or rubber bands to hold the figures together until the glue dries.

Make a group of Pilgrims and Native Americans to decorate your table this Thanksgiving.

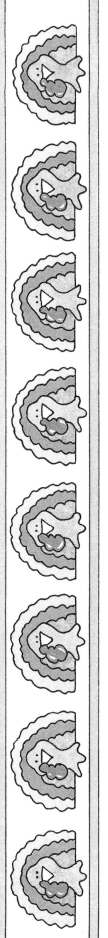

The Pilgrims and the Native Americans celebrated the first Thanksgiving with a big meal called a feast.

A Movable Feast

Here is what you need:

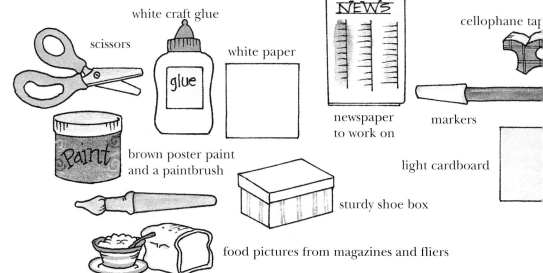

white craft glue

scissors

white paper

cellophane tape

newspaper to work on

markers

brown poster paint and a paintbrush

light cardboard

sturdy shoe box

food pictures from magazines and fliers

Here is what you do:

1 Turn the shoe box upside down and cut a rectangle-shaped piece out of each side of the box. The remaining corner pieces should now look like the legs of a table.

2 Paint the box-table brown and let it dry.

3 Make food for the table by drawing some with markers on the white paper or by cutting pictures from magazines or grocery fliers.

4 Glue the cutout food pictures to light cardboard and let them dry. Cover the front of the food pictures with strips of cellophane tape to protect them.

5 Draw a tab on the bottom of each food item to use to insert it in the table. Cut the food out.

6 Use a marker to mark slits on the table where you would like to set the food. Cut the slits you have marked.

7 Slide the food tabs into the slits to stand the food on the table for a big feast.

You don't have to make all the food for your table at once. You can add more food over time. It is fun to collect different meals to "set your table."

The Pilgrims and the Native Americans feasted on wild turkey at the first Thanksgiving.

Wild, Bouncy Turkey

Here is what you need:

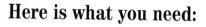

scissors

orange and red pipe cleaners

two wiggle eyes

brown and orange construction paper scra[p]

white craft glue

glue

corrugated box cardboard

pen

craft feathers

large rubber band

ruler

Here is what you do:

1. Use the pen to draw two 4- to 5-inch (10- to 13-cm) circles on the corrugated cardboard. You might want to trace around the rim of a plastic container or lid to get an even circle. For a fancy turkey, you can scallop the edge of the front circle, but you don't need to.

2. Fold a 12-inch (30-cm) orange pipe cleaner in half to make legs for the turkey. Cut a 1-inch (2.5-cm) piece from each end of the pipe cleaner. Wrap a piece around the pipe cleaner near the end of each leg to make feet. Bend the feet forward. Cut the legs apart at the bend.

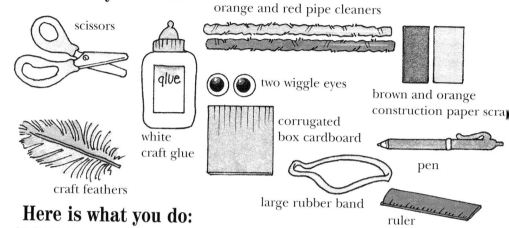

3. Cut the rubber band and flatten it into one long strip of elastic. Glue the two cardboard circles together with the front circle slightly lower than the back one, the rubber band caught between them as shown on the following page. It is important that the groove lines of the cardboard run up and down so that the holes formed by the grooves are at the top of the project.

4 Slide the top of each leg into a hole formed by the grooves in the bottom of the front circle. Secure with a dab of glue.

5 Cut a head for the turkey from the brown paper. Glue the head to the front of the turkey.

6 Cut a triangle-shaped beak for the turkey from the orange paper. Glue the beak to the head of the turkey.

7 Wrap a piece of red pipe cleaner around your finger to make a wattle for the turkey. Glue the red wattle under the beak.

8 Glue the two wiggle eyes to the head of the turkey above the beak.

9 Stick a feather inside the front cardboard circle on each side of the turkey for wings.

10 Stick lots of feathers in the groove holes at the top of both the front and back cardboard circles to give the turkey a colorful tail.

Hang the turkey or bounce it around the room on the end of the elastic band.

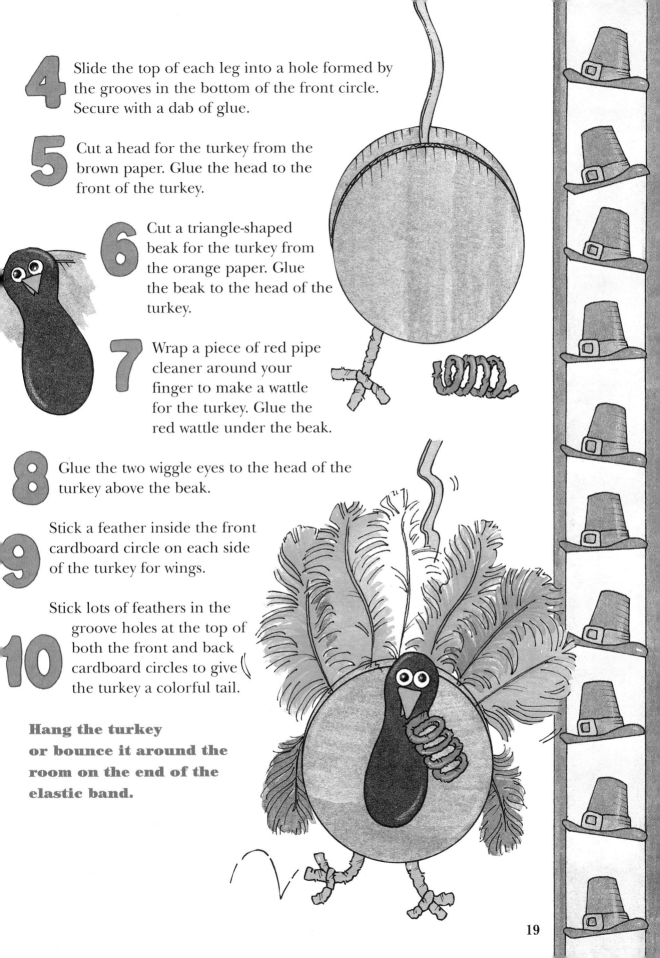

**On Thanksgiving we remember to give thanks
for our friends and our family.**

Gift of Friends and Family

Here is what you need:

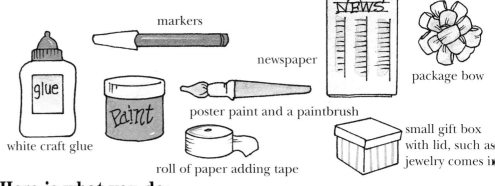

markers

newspaper

package bow

glue

white craft glue

Paint

poster paint and a paintbrush

roll of paper adding tape

small gift box with lid, such as jewelry comes in

Here is what you do:

1 Paint the outside of the gift box and lid.

2 Glue the bow on the lid.

3 Tear off a strip of paper adding tape long enough to draw the faces of your family and friends. If you don't have adding tape, cut strips of paper and tape them together using cellophane tape.

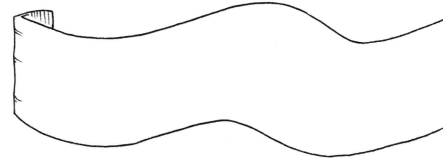

4 Use the markers to draw the family and friends you are thankful for this Thanksgiving.

5 Glue the back of one end of the strip inside the bottom of the box.

6 Carefully fold the strip back and forth accordion style to make it fit neatly inside the gift box. Glue the back of the other end of the strip to the inside of the lid.

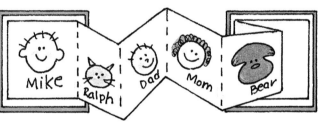

The pictures can be displayed by opening the gift box, pulling the strip out, and turning the box and lid on one side to support the two ends of the picture strip.

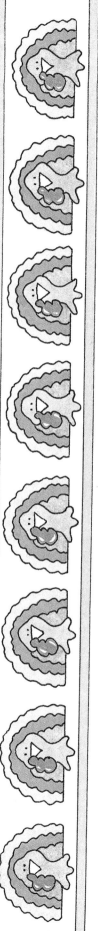

On Thanksgiving we remember to give thanks for our homes.

Home Sweet Home Sampler

Here is what you need:

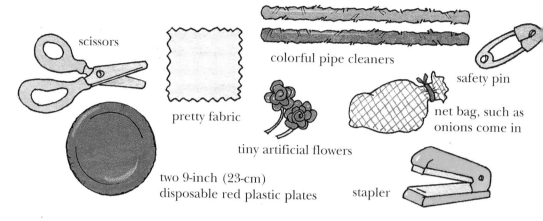

scissors

pretty fabric

colorful pipe cleaners

safety pin

tiny artificial flowers

net bag, such as onions come in

two 9-inch (23-cm) disposable red plastic plates

stapler

Here is what you do:

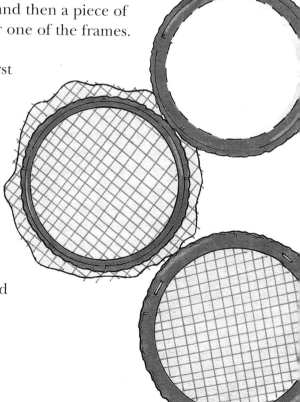

1 Cut the centers out of both plates, leaving the outer rims for a frame.

2 Stretch a piece of fabric and then a piece of net cut from the bag over one of the frames.

3 Cover the edges of the first frame with the second frame so that the net and fabric are between the two rims.

4 Staple the two frames together, pulling the fabric and net tight across the frame as you go around. Trim the excess fabric and net from around the outside of the frame.

HOME SWEET HOME

5 Cut pieces of pipe cleaner to spell out "Home Sweet Home."

6 Weave the pipe-cleaner letters through the netting to attach them to the framed fabric.

7 Pin a safety pin to the back top edge of the fabric for a hanger.

8 Tuck some tiny artificial flowers in the netting around the letters and to cover the bar of the safety pin.

A long time ago young girls and women sewed "samplers"— letters and pictures stitched on fabric—that said "Home Sweet Home."

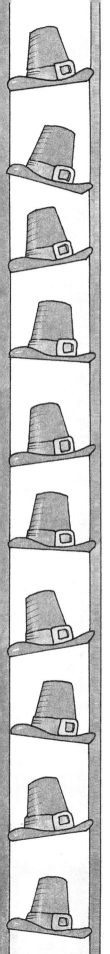

On Thanksgiving we remember to give thanks for our food.

Recipe Card Box

Here is what you need:

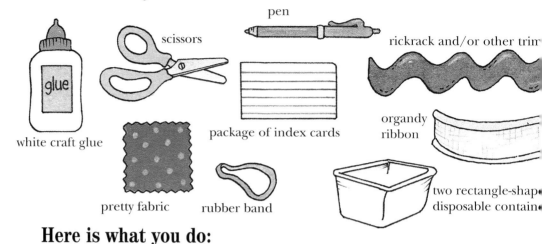

glue

white craft glue

scissors

pen

package of index cards

rickrack and/or other trim

organdy ribbon

pretty fabric

rubber band

two rectangle-shaped disposable containers

Here is what you do:

1 Cut a piece of fabric large enough to entirely cover the outside of the container. Tuck the excess fabric inside.

2 Hold the fabric in place over the bottom of the container by placing the rubber band around the edge of the container.

3 Turn the container back over and glue the edges of the fabric inside the container. Push the second container down inside the first one to hold the fabric in place.

4 Tie a piece of ribbon in a bow around the top edge of the container.

5 The index cards can be placed in the container to use to write recipes. You can make tabs for different types of food with some of the cards. Make three tabs at a time. Turn the cards over to the blank side if they have one. Write the first category, maybe Main Dishes, at the top left side of the first card. Then cut away the remaining strip at the top of the card after the writing.

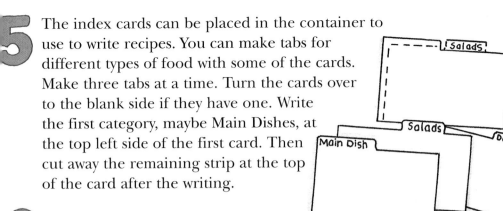

6 Hold the first card over the second card and write the next category, maybe Salads, in the center at the top of the card. Cut away the strip of card on each side of the writing.

7 For the last card hold the second card over it and write the category at the top to the right, where the strip has been cut from the second card.

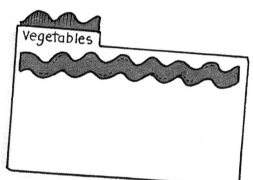

8 Making the tabs in groups of three this way will make them easier to read in the recipe box, because the tabs won't block one another.

9 Glue a line of rickrack or trim behind each tab and sticking up to make the categories easier to find. Glue another line of trim across the card and below the tab to make it look nice.

You might want to find some recipes in old magazines or online that sound good to you. Write them on the cards. A recipe box makes a great gift for someone you know who likes to cook.

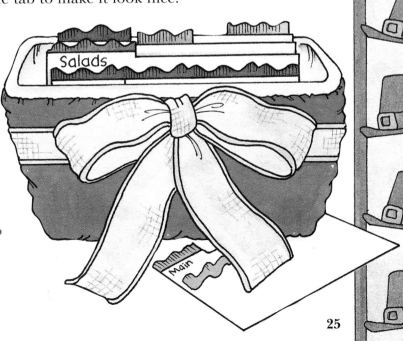

Fall gourds make wonderful table turkeys.

Gourd Turkeys

Here is what you need:

one or more gourds

craft feathers

white craft glue

red pipe cleaner

glue

colored-ball map pins

Here is what you do:

1 Turn a gourd on one side. The stem of the gourd will become the beak of the turkey. Wrap a piece of red pipe cleaner around your finger to make a wattle for the turkey. Wrap the end of the wattle around the stem beak so that it hangs down from the beak.

2 Push two map pins into the gourd above the beak for the eyes.

3 Push two map pins halfway into the gourd on the bottom side to become legs and support the gourd turkey in standing.

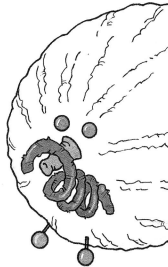

4 Glue a craft feather on each side of the gourd for wings.

5 Glue several colorful craft feathers sticking up from the back of the turkey (the bottom of the gourd) for tail feathers.

Bet you can't make just one! Try using gourds in a variety of different shapes and colors to make a flock of turkeys.

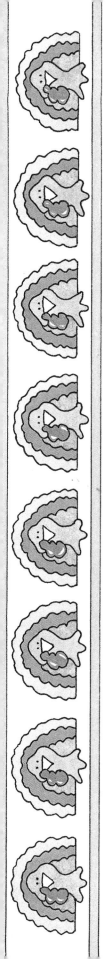

The cornucopia has become a Thanksgiving symbol of abundance

Table Cornucopia

Here is what you need:

scissors

white craft glue

glue

colored tissue paper

old CD

solid color cone-shaped party hat

brown and yellow pipe cleaners

organdy ribbon

green construction paper scrap

five or more red, green, and orange plastic soda twist-off c...

purple, red, and brown craft beads

Here is what you do:

1 Turn the party hat on one side and fold the tip of the hat up to make the cornucopia.

2 Cut a square of colorful tissue paper to push into the cornucopia as a lining. Secure the tissue paper to the inside of the hat with glue, letting the paper stick out around the edges.

3 Crumble a ball of the same color tissue paper and glue it inside the cornucopia to provide a place to glue the "fruits" you will make. Glue the cornucopia to the silver side of the CD.

4 Tie a large bow from the organdy ribbon. Glue the bow to one side of the top of the cornucopia.

5 If any of the plastic caps you are using have writing on the top, cover the writing with paper (or paint) that is the same color as the cap. Use the red and green caps to make apples. Glue a piece of brown pipe cleaner on the edge for the apple stem. Add a tiny leaf cut from the green construction paper.

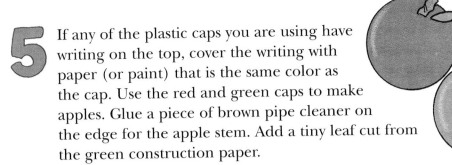

6 Use the orange caps to make oranges. Fold a tiny piece of brown pipe cleaner in half and glue it to the top edge to look like the end of an orange.

7 To make grapes, thread several purple craft beads on a piece of brown pipe cleaner. Fold and squeeze the pipe cleaner to look like a bunch of grapes.

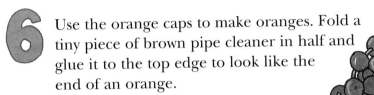

8 Fold a yellow pipe cleaner back and forth. Squeeze the folded ends together on each side to make bananas.

9 Arrange all the fruits inside the cornucopia, covering the crumpled tissue backing inside the hat and spilling out onto the CD.

10 Glue groups of nuts (brown craft beads) and berries (red craft beads) among the larger fruits.

You might have ideas for making other kinds of fruits to add to your cornucopia.

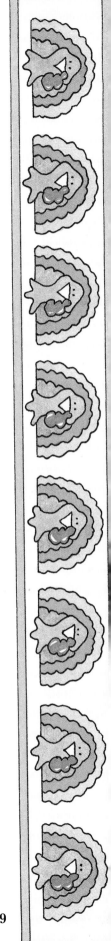

This turkey project is so easy you can make a basketful in no time at all.

A Bow-tiful Turkey

Here is what you need:

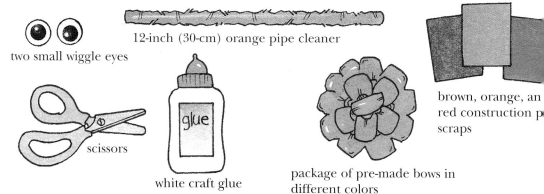

two small wiggle eyes

12-inch (30-cm) orange pipe cleaner

scissors

white craft glue

package of pre-made bows in different colors

brown, orange, an[d] red construction p[aper] scraps

Here is what you do:

1 Glue two different color bows of similar size together, bottom to bottom, to make the body of the turkey.

2 Bend the orange pipe cleaner in half. Cut a 1-inch (2.5-cm) piece off each end. Wrap one of the pieces around each end of the folded pipe cleaner, about an inch from the end, to become toes. Bend the toes forward for the feet of the turkey.

3 Glue the pipe cleaner feet around the center of the two joined bows so that the feet stick out at the bottom of the turkey.

4 Cut a head for the turkey from the brown construction paper.

5 Cut a triangle-shaped beak from the orange construction paper. Glue the beak to the head of the turkey.

6 Cut a wattle from the red construction paper. Glue the wattle to the head of the turkey just below the beak.

7 Glue the two wiggle eyes to the head above the beak.

8 Glue the head to the front of the turkey.

Try making several turkeys using different combinations of colors for the bow bodies, then flock them together in the center or scatter them across your Thanksgiving table.

If you are having lots of company at your house for Thanksgiving, might want to use place cards to tell each person where to sit

Pilgrim Place Cards

Here is what you need:

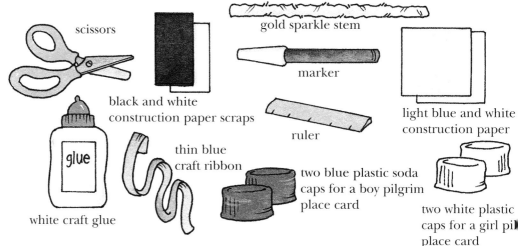

scissors

gold sparkle stem

black and white construction paper scraps

marker

ruler

light blue and white construction paper

thin blue craft ribbon

two blue plastic soda caps for a boy pilgrim place card

two white plastic caps for a girl pil place card

white craft glue

glue

Here is what you do:

1 To make the boy pilgrim place card, glue two blue caps together, one on top of the other for the hat. (If any of the plastic caps you are using have writing on the top, cover the writing with paper or paint that is the same color as the cap.)

2 Cut a circle from the black paper slightly bigger around than the caps for the brim of the hat.

3 Glue the caps to the center of the brim.

4 Glue a piece of blue ribbon around the cap just above the brim for the hatband. Make a buckle for the hatband by folding a piece of sparkle stem into a small square. Glue the buckle to the hatband.

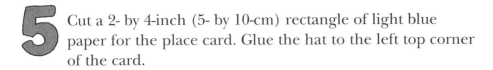

5 Cut a 2- by 4-inch (5- by 10-cm) rectangle of light blue paper for the place card. Glue the hat to the left top corner of the card.

6 To make the girl pilgrim place card, glue two white caps together, one on top of the other. Turn the caps on one side for the bonnet.

7 Cut a rectangle of white paper to just cover the top and sides of the bonnet. Glue the paper over the bonnet, folding the corners out on each side.

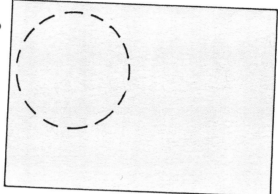

8 Cut a 2- by 4-inch (5-by 10-cm) rectangle of light blue paper for the place card. Glue the hat to the top left corner of the card. Tie a piece of craft ribbon in a tiny bow. Glue the bow on the card at the bottom front of the bonnet.

On the blue paper rectangle, use the marker to write the name of the person the place card is for.

33

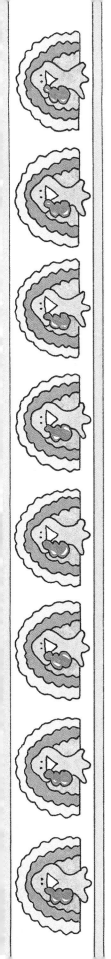

Lots of these clever napkin rings can be made in no time at all!

Turkey Napkin Ring

Here is what you need:

scissors

two wiggle eyes

orange felt scrap

white craft glue

red pipe cleaner

paper clip

ruler

old necktie

clamp clothespin

Here is what you do:

1. Measuring from the point, cut a 7-inch (18-cm) piece from the narrow end of the necktie.

2. Wrap the piece around in a circle so that the point overlaps the outside of the cut end.

3. Secure the point with glue. Use a clamp clothespin to hold the two ends of the tie together until the glue dries.

4. Cut a triangle beak for the turkey from the orange felt. Glue the beak over the point of the tie.

5 Glue the two wiggle eyes above the beak.

6 Wrap a piece of red pipe cleaner around your finger to curl it to make the wattle. Glue one end of the wattle under the beak.

To use the napkin ring, fold a napkin like a fan and slide it through the ring. Bring the two ends of the napkin up to meet and secure them from the top with a paper clip. The fanned napkin will become the tail of the turkey.

Make a surprise for each Thanksgiving guest.

Tom-tom Favor

Here is what you need:

yarn or rickrack

scissors

craft feathers

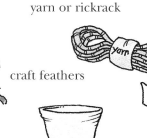

pony beads

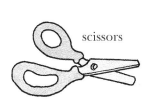

empty plastic fruit
or pudding snack cup

two colorful 12-inch
(30-cm) balloons

candy or small surprises

Here is what you do:

1 Cut the neck off the two balloons.

2 Fill the snack cup partway with candy or other small surprises. If it is too full you will not be able to shake it and hear the drum sound.

3 Pull one balloon over the top of the cup and down the sides to close the opening.

4 Pull the other balloon over the bottom of the snack cup and up the sides over the first balloon to cover the outside of the cup.

5 Wrap the edge of the top of the drum with yarn or rickrack and tie the ends together to secure.

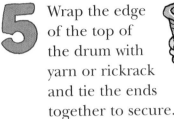

6 If you use yarn you might want to string a few beads on the ends of the yarn to hang down off the top side of the drum.

7 Tuck one or two craft feathers into the yarn or trim.

The drum will need to be taken apart to get the candy out. If you want to make a drum to keep, omit the candy and add some beads to the cup to make the drum sound.

An extra trivet or two will be a welcome gift for a hostess serving lots of yoummy Thanksgiving food.

Stick Trivet

Here is what you need:

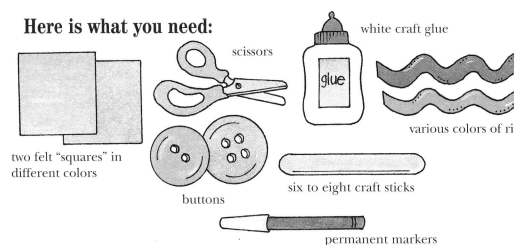

scissors

white craft glue

glue

various colors of ri

two felt "squares" in different colors

buttons

six to eight craft sticks

permanent markers

Here is what you do:

1 Make one of the felt pieces a true square by trimming off one side. (Most felt "squares" are really rectangles.)

2 Cut a square from the second color of felt that is about 1 inch (2.5 cm) smaller than the first square.

3 Fold the smaller square in half and cut nine slits across it without cutting through the edge of the felt.

4 You can color one side of the sticks with the markers or leave the sticks the natural color.

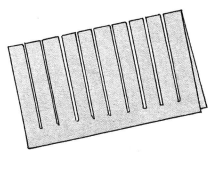

5 Weave as many sticks as you can into the slits of the small square by weaving the first stick over then under the felt until you reach the other side. The next stick must start by going under the felt that the first stick went over.

6 When you have woven sticks all the way across the felt, glue the stick mat to the center of the larger square of felt.

7 Glue rickrack trims and/or buttons around the edges of the trivet to decorate it.

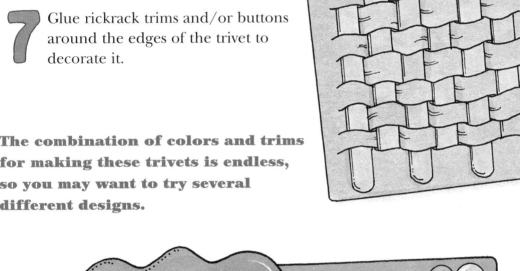

The combination of colors and trims for making these trivets is endless, so you may want to try several different designs.

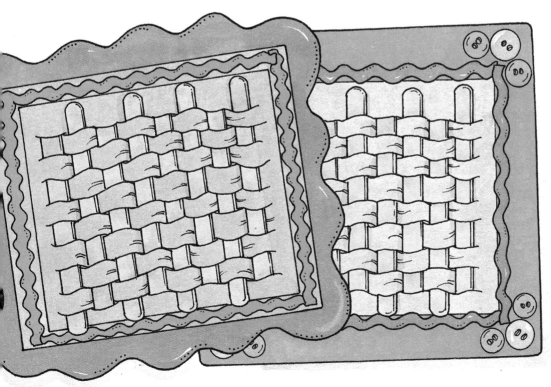

Get everyone into the Thanksgiving spirit by making this festive turkey to hang on the door.

Turkey Wreath

Here is what you need:

two wiggle eyes

scissors

red pipe cleaner

orange felt scra[p]

cellophane tape

large paper clip and several regular-size paper clips

two 9-inch (23-cm) uncoated paper plates

red cone-shaped party hat (or paint one red)

glue

white craft glue

package of pre-made bows

Here is what you do:

1 Cut the center out of both paper plates so that you are left with the outer rings. Glue them together to make one ring that is sturdier.

2 Cut four 2-inch (5-cm) slits, about an inch apart, in the rim on one side of the hat. Fold the tab on each end forward for the legs for the turkey. Cut toes in the end of each tab. Cut away the center tab and a small amount of the hat on each side.

3 Cut slits about 2 inches (5 cm) apart and halfway up the remainder of the hat. Fold the tabs up to form the tail for the turkey.

4 Fold the tip of the party hat forward toward the legs to make the head of the turkey.

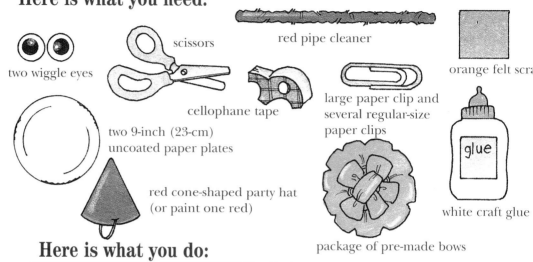

5 Cut a triangle-shaped beak from the orange felt. Glue the beak to the front of the point of the head. Glue the two wiggle eyes to the head above the beak.

6 Wrap a piece of red pipe cleaner around your finger to curl it for the wattle. Glue one end of the wattle to the tip of the hat behind the beak so that it hangs down from the head.

7 Glue the back of the turkey to the bottom of the wreath ring so that the ring becomes part of the tail.

8 Glue the end of the large paper clip to the back of the wreath and secure it with cellophane tape. The end of the large paper clip should be sticking up to make the hanger for the wreath.

9 Glue colorful bows all over the wreath ring and the tail of the turkey. Use paper clips to secure any loose bows until the glue dries.

Gobble! Gobble!

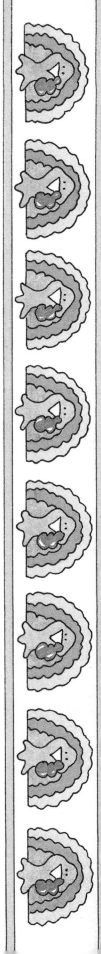

Make this puzzle to do yourself and share with holiday visitors.

Rubber Band Thanksgiving Puzzle

Here is what you need:

scissors

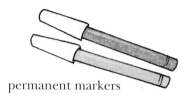

permanent markers

stiff box cardboard

sixteen or more flat, identical rubber bands

Here is what you do:

1 Cut a rectangle of cardboard that is just wide enough to slide the rubber bands on and hold them without stretching them too much. Make the card a couple of inches longer than it is tall.

2 Slide all the rubber bands onto the cardboard so that they are flat and side by side with the edges touching.

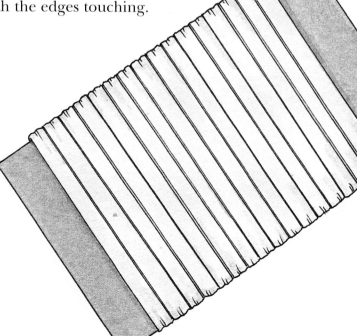

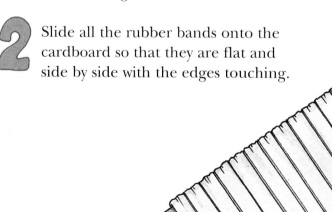

3 Use the markers to draw a Thanksgiving picture on the rubber-band surface on one side of the cardboard.

4 Turn the cardboard over and draw a different picture on the other side.

To do the puzzle, remove all the rubber bands, mix them up, and try to put the two pictures back together again on the card.

Any small child will be thankful for this project that helps hold and display playing cards.

Turkey Playing Cards Holder

Here is what you need:

scissors

white craft glue

glue

red and orange pipe cleaners

bump chenille pipe cleaners

corrugated cardboard

seed beads

ballpoint pen

playing cards

Here is what you do:

1 Cut two identical 4-inch (10-cm) circles from the corrugated cardboard. Hold them together and use the ballpoint pen to poke through the center of both circles.

2 Cut two bumps from the bump chenille pipe cleaner. You will use a bump on each side of the holder to make two turkey heads.

3 Thread the strip of chenille through the center holes in the two circles so that there is one bump on each side and the two circles are held together. Bend the two bumps up on each side, then fold the ends forward to look like turkey heads.

4 Cut a 2-inch (5-cm) piece of red pipe cleaner to make a wattle for each turkey head. Curl one end of each piece around the pen, then wrap the other end around the neck of the turkey to secure it with the curled end hanging down. Glue two beads on each turkey head for the eyes.

5 Turn one of the corrugated cardboard circles so that the holes are at the bottom of the turkey.

6 Cut two 3-inch (7.5-cm) pieces of orange pipe cleaner for the legs of the turkey. Dip one end of each leg into the glue, then slide the end up into one of the holes at the bottom of the turkey. Put each leg in a different hole about 1 inch (2.5 cm) apart.

7 Cut two 1-inch (2.5-cm) pieces of orange pipe cleaner to wrap around the bottom part of each leg for toes.

To use the turkey card holder, slip the cards between the two turkeys so that the fanned out cards forms the tail of the turkey.

These fun and festive rings make wonderful table favors.

Indian Headband Rings

Here is what you need:

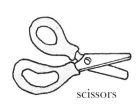

scissors

white craft glue

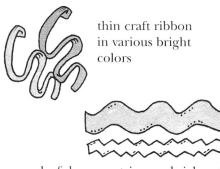

thin craft ribbon in various bright colors

colorful narrow trims and rick-rack

Here is what you do:

1 Cut a piece of trim or rick-rack long enough to fit around the finger of the person wearing the ring and then overlap a tiny bit.

2 Glue the cut trim into a circle to make the ring.

3 To make a feather for the headband ring, cut a 1-inch (2.5-cm) piece of craft ribbon. Cut one end of the ribbon to a point.

Cut slits along each side of the ribbon to make it resemble a feather.

5 Glue the uncut end of the ribbon feather to the inside of the ring.

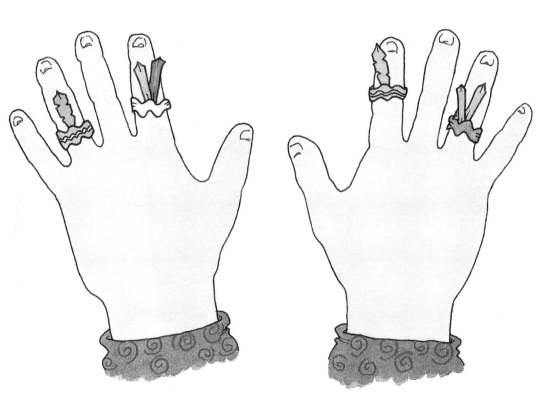

These rings are so quick and easy to make you could easily make one for everyone in your class as a Thanksgiving surprise.

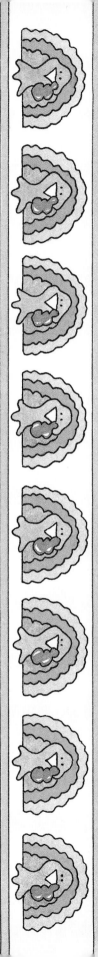

About the Author and Artist

Thirty years as a teacher and director of nursery school programs have given Kathy Ross extensive experience in guiding young children through craft projects. Among the more than forty craft books she has written are *Crafts for All Seasons*, *The Storytime Craft Book*, *Things to Make for Your Doll*, and *Star-Spangled Crafts*. To find out more about Kathy, visit her Website: www.Kathyross.com.

Sharon Lane Holm, a resident of Fairfield, Connecticut, won awards for her work in advertising design before shifting her concentration to children's books. Her recent books include *Happy New Year, Everywhere!* and *Merry Christmas, Everywhere!*, by Arlene Erlbach. You can see more of her work at www.sharonholm.com.

Together, Kathy Ross and Sharon Lane Holm have created *The Best Christmas Crafts Ever!* and *The Big Book of Christian Crafts*, as well as two earlier books in this series: *All New Crafts for Easter*, and *All New Crafts for Halloween*.